POPULAR IRISH POETRY

Popular Irish Poetry

SELECTED AND INTRODUCED
BY LOUIS BELL

Gill & Macmillan

Gill & Macmillan Ltd
Goldenbridge
Dublin 8
with associated companies throughout the world
© Selection and introduction Louis Bell 1995
0 7171 2270 0
Illustrations by Fiona Fewer
Print origination by Identikit Design Consultants, Dublin
Printed by ColourBooks Ltd, Dublin

A catalogue record is available for this book
from the British Library.

1 3 5 4 2

Contents

Introduction

CECIL FRANCES ALEXANDER (1818–95)
All Things Bright and Beautiful 11
Calvary 12
ANONYMOUS
Kilcash 13
The Night Before Larry Was Stretched 14
WILLIAM ALLINGHAM (1824–89)
Four Ducks on a Pond 17
The Fairies 17
HELEN SELINA BLACKWOOD (1807–87)
The Irish Emigrant 19
JEREMIAH JOSEPH CALLANAN (1795–1829)
The Convict of Clonmel 21
JOHN KEEGAN CASEY (1846–70)
The Rising of the Moon 22
AUSTIN CLARKE (1896–1974)
Burial of an Irish President 24
PÁDRAIC COLUM (1881–1972)
The Old Woman of the Roads 25
A Drover 26
THOMAS DAVIS (1814–45)
The West's Asleep 27
My Land 28
SIR AUBREY DE VERE (1788–1846)
The Rock of Cashel 29
PAUL DURCAN (1944–)
On the Floor at the Foot of the Bed 30
Going Home to Mayo 31
Backside to the Wind 32
SAMUEL FERGUSON (1810–86)
The Lark in the Clear Air 34
OLIVER GOLDSMITH (1728–74)
The Deserted Village 35

EVA GORE-BOOTH (1870–1926)
The Little Waves of Breffny   36
GERALD GRIFFIN (1803–40)
Hy-Brazil — the Isle of the Blest   37
SEAMUS HEANEY (1939–)
Digging   38
Blackberry-Picking   40
North   41
The Toome Road   42
Exposure   43
JOHN KELLS INGRAM (1823–1907)
The Memory of the Dead   45
JAMES JOYCE (1882–1941)
Ecce Puer   46
The Ballad of Persse O'Reilly   47
PATRICK KAVANAGH (1905–67)
Shancoduff   49
Epic   50
Canal Bank Walk   51
Lines Written on a Seat ...   51
In Memory of my Mother   52
On Raglan Road   53
BRENDAN KENNELLY (1936–)
My Dark Fathers   54
FRANCIS LEDWIDGE (1887–1917)
June   56
Thomas MacDonagh   57
LOUIS MACNEICE (1907–63)
The Sunlight on the Garden   57
DEREK MAHON (1941–)
A Disused Shed in Co. Wexford   58
JAMES CLARENCE MANGAN (1803–49)
Dark Rosaleen   60
THOMAS MOORE (1779–1852)
Let Erin Remember   63
The Light of Other Days   64
She is Far from the Land   65
The Harp that Once through Tara's Halls   65

NUALA NÍ DHOMHNAILL (1952–)
  I Fall in Love   66
JOHN BOYLE O'REILLY (1844–90)
  A White Rose   67
EILEEN O'LEARY (c.1743–1800)
  The Lament for Art O'Leary   67
PATRICK PEARSE (1879–1916)
  The Wayfarer   69
JOSEPH MARY PLUNKETT (1887–1916)
  The Presence of God   69
FR PROUT (F.S. MAHONY, 1804–66)
  The Shandon Bells   70
JAMES STEPHENS (c.1882–1950)
  The Snare   72
JOHNATHAN SWIFT (1667–1745)
  Stella's Birthday   73
KATHARINE TYNAN (1861–1931)
  Sheep and Lambs   76
  The Wind that Shakes the Barley   77
EDWARD WALSH (1805–50)
  The Dawning of the Day   78
OSCAR WILDE (1854–1900)
  The Ballad of Reading Gaol   79
W.B. YEATS (1865–1939)
  The Lake Isle of Innisfree   80
  The Stolen Child   81
  When You Are Old   83
  The Song of Wandering Aengus   83
  He Wishes for the Cloths of Heaven   84
  Red Hanrahan's Song About Ireland   85
  No Second Troy   86
  September 1913   86
  The Wild Swans at Coole   87
  The Stare's Nest by My Window   89
  In Memory of Eva Gore-Booth and
    Con Markiewicz   90
  Under Ben Bulben   91

Index of First Lines   93
Acknowledgments   96

Introduction

This little book is not a selection of the best in Irish poetry, or even of my own favourite poems. While it contains some work that would qualify under either heading, it tries to stay faithful to the book's title. It is popular poetry, by which I mean verse that has established itself in the public affection.

The presence of such a large body of genuinely popular poetry — only a fraction of which is represented here — must account in part for the fact that Ireland is such a fertile source of new verse, whether of high or low degree. Traditions of rote learning and public recitation helped to keep poetry flourishing in Ireland, until meeting the disapproval of most educational theorists of the last thirty years or so. Although these practices are being subverted, they have been replaced in part by public readings all across the country which bear witness to the continuing strength of poetry as a public art.

I was tempted to arrange this selection in the traditional chronological way, by each poet's date of birth. In a bigger anthology, this would have the merit of showing the stylistic and thematic development of Irish poetry over the centuries. A small book can, however, only give a rough cross-section of Irish poetic sensibility and in the end I thought that the wholly random criterion of poets' surnames was as good a principle as any other. It means that *Popular Irish Poetry* is not so much nouvelle cuisine as an old-fashioned Irish stew, with all sorts of things chucked in together cheek by jowl.

Readers will easily spot common themes for themselves. Much Irish poetry before Yeats was dominated by the public rhetoric of patriotism, expressed

either in overtly political terms or in a lyricism that
celebrated countryside and people. Yeats deepened this
tradition, gave it its fullest expression, and then moved
beyond it to the poetry of his later years in which
mystical, philosophical and personal concerns loomed
larger. This great genius is not just Ireland's national poet.
He is one who, like Beethoven, inherits a tradition,
exhausts and transforms it, setting a new agenda for all
who follow. The shadow of Yeats may sometimes be
oppressive to the poets who have succeeded him but that
in itself is a measure of his colossal achievement.

The generation after Yeats had the misfortune
to live in the leaden age of censorship. Those years are
recalled in Austin Clarke's acidulous poem on the funeral
of President Douglas Hyde. In what was a cold climate for
poetry, only the work of Patrick Kavanagh really
impinged on the wider public. Kavanagh and Clarke both
lived to see the extraordinary re-birth of Irish poetry from
the late sixties on. Yet either would have been amazed
and perhaps a little envious at the positions of status
and prestige now accorded in Ireland to Irish poets
and their work.

It is as if Ireland is over-compensating for the years
of censorship by the brilliance of its second literary
revival. Irish drama, fiction and poetry have not only
swept the world: they have liberated a new generation
of Irish people into a renewal of one of the island's
oldest traditions.

The last thirty years have yielded a very different
kind of poetry to that traditionally labelled 'popular'.
In this little anthology, one only has to see Seamus
Heaney squeezed in between Gerald Griffin and John
Kells Ingram to appreciate the point. Yet, happily, there
is a place for them all in this particular Irish stew.
Bon appetit!

CECIL FRANCES ALEXANDER

All Things Bright and Beautiful

All things bright and beautiful,
All creatures great and small,
All things wise and wonderful,
The Lord God made them all.

Each little flower that opens,
Each little bird that sings,
He made their glowing colours,
He made their tiny wings.

The rich man in his castle,
The poor man at his gate,
God made them high or lowly,
And ordered their estate.

The purple-headed mountain,
The river running by,
The sunset and the morning,
That brightens up the sky;

The cold wind in the winter,
The pleasant summer sun,
The ripe fruits in the garden—
He made them every one.

The tall trees in the greenwood,
The meadows where we play,
The rushes by the water
We gather every day;

He gave us eyes to see them,
And lips that we might tell,
How great is God Almighty,
Who has made all things well.

CECIL FRANCES ALEXANDER

Calvary

There is a green hill far away
Without a city wall,
Where the dear Lord was crucified
Who died to save us all.

We may not know, we cannot tell
What pains He had to bear,
But we do know it was for us
He hung and suffered there.

He died that we might be forgiven,
He died to make us good,
That we might go at last to Heaven,
Saved by His Precious Blood.

There was none other good enough
To pay the price of sin;
He only could unlock the gate
Of Heaven and let us in.

O, dearly, dearly has He loved,
And we must love Him too
With all our strength and all our mind,
And prove our love is true.

ANONYMOUS

Kilcash

What shall we do for timber?
    The last of the woods is down.
Kilcash and the house of its glory
    And the bell of the house are gone,
The spot where that lady waited
    Who shamed all women for grace
When earls came sailing to greet her
    And Mass was said in the place.

My grief and my affliction
    Your gates are taken away,
Your avenue needs attention,
    Goats in the garden stray.
The courtyard's filled with water
    And the great earls where are they?
The earls, the lady, the people
    Beaten into the clay.

No sound of duck or geese there,
    Hawk's cry or eagle's call,
No humming of the bees there
    That brought honey and wax for all,
Nor even the sound of the birds there
    When the sun goes down in the west,
No cuckoo on top of the boughs there,
    Singing the world to rest.

There's mist there tumbling from branches,
    Unstirred by night and by day,
And darkness falling from heaven,
    For our fortune has ebbed away,

There's no holly nor hazel nor ash there,
　　The pasture's rock and stone,
The crown of the forest has withered,
　　And the last of its game is gone.

I beseech of Mary and Jesus
　　That the great come home again
With long dances danced in the garden,
　　Fiddle music and mirth among men,
That Kilcash the home of our fathers
　　Be lifted on high again,
And from that to the deluge of waters
　　In bounty and peace remain.

(Translated from the original Irish by Frank O'Connor)

ANONYMOUS

The Night Before Larry Was Stretched

The night before Larry was stretched,
　　The boys they all paid him a visit;
A bait in their sacks, too, they fetched;
　　They sweated their duds till they riz it:
For Larry was ever the lad,
　　When a boy was condemned to the squeezer,
Would fence all the duds that he had
　　To help a poor friend to a sneezer,
　　　　And warm his gob 'fore he died.

The boys they came crowding in fast,
　　Till they drew all their stools round about him,
Six glims round his trap-case were placed,
　　He couldn't be waked well without 'em.

When one of us asked could he die
 Without having duly repented,
Says Larry, 'That's all in my eye;
 And first by the clargy invented,
  To get a fat bit for themselves.'

'I'm sorry, dear Larry,' says I,
 'to see you in this situation;
And, blister my limbs if I lie,
 I'd as lieve it had been my own station.'
'Ochone! it's all over,' says he,
 'For the neckcloth I'll be forced to put on
And by this time tomorrow you'll see
 Your poor Larry as dead as a mutton,
  Because, why, his courage was good.

'And I'll be cut up like a pie,
 And my nob from my body be parted.'
'You're in the wrong box, then,' says I,
 'For blast me if they're so hard-hearted:
A chalk on the back of your neck
 Is all that Jack Ketch cares to give you;
Then mind not such trifles a feck,
 For why should the likes of them grieve you?
  And now, boys, come tip us the deck.'

The cards being called for, they played,
 Till Larry found one of them cheated;
A dart at his napper he made
 (The boy being easily heated):
'Oh, by the hokey, you thief,
 I'll scuttle your nob with my daddle!
You cheat me because I'm in grief
 But soon I'll demolish your noddle,
  And leave you your claret to drink.'

Then the clergy came in with his book,
  He spoke him so smooth and so civil;
Larry tipped him a Kilmainham look,
  And pitched his big wig to the devil:
Then sighing, he threw back his head
  To get a sweet drop of the bottle,
And pitiful sighing, he said:
   'Oh, the hemp will be soon round my throttle
    And choke my poor windpipe to death.

'Though sure it's the best way to die,
  Oh, the devil a better-a-livin'!
For, sure, when the gallows is high
  Your journey is shorter to Heaven:
But what harasses Larry the most,
  And makes his poor soul melancholy,
Is to think of the time when his ghost
   Will come in a sheet to sweet Molly —
    Oh, sure it will kill her alive!'

So moving these last words he spoke,
  We all vented our tears in a shower;
For my part, I thought my heart broke,
  To see him cut down like a flower.
On his travels we watched him next day;
  Oh, the throttler, I thought I could kill him;
But Larry not one word did say,
   Nor changed till he come to 'King William' —
    Then, *musha*! his colour grew white.

When he came to the nubbling chit,
  He was tucked up so neat and so pretty,
The rumbler jogged off from his feet,
  And he died with his face to the city;

He kicked, too — but that was all pride,
    For soon you might see 'twas all over;
Soon after the noose was untied,
    And at darky we waked him in clover,
        And sent him to take a ground sweat.

WILLIAM ALLINGHAM

Four Ducks on a Pond

Four ducks on a pond,
A grass-bank beyond,
A blue sky of spring,
White clouds on the wing:
Ah, what a small thing
To remember for years —
To remember with tears!

WILLIAM ALLINGHAM

The Fairies

Up the airy mountain
Down the rushy glen,
We daren't go a-hunting
For fear of little men;
Wee folk, good folk,
Trooping all together;
Green jacket, red cap,
And white owl's feather.

Down along the rocky shore
Some make their home —
They live on crispy pancakes
Of yellow tide foam;
Some in the reeds
Of the black mountain lake,
With frogs for their watch-dogs,
All night awake.

By the craggy hillside,
Through the mosses bare,
They have planted thorn trees
For pleasure here and there.
Is any man so daring
As dig one up in spite,
He shall find their sharpest thorns
In his bed at night.

Up the airy mountain,
Down the rushy glen,
We daren't go a hunting
For fear of little men;
Wee folk, good folk,
Trooping all together;
Green jacket, red cap,
And white owl's feather!

HELEN SELINA BLACKWOOD

The Irish Emigrant

I'm sitting on the stile, Mary,
    Where we sat, side by side,
That bright May morning long ago
    When first you were my bride.
The corn was springing fresh and green,
    The lark sang loud and high,
The red was on your lip, Mary,
    The love-light in your eye.

The place is little changed, Mary,
    The day is bright as then,
The lark's loud song is in my ear,
    The corn is green again;
But I miss the soft clasp of your hand,
    Your breath warm on my cheek,
And I still keep list'ning for the words
    You never more may speak.

'Tis but a step down yonder lane,
    The little Church stands near —
The Church where we were wed, Mary —
    I see the spire from here;
But the graveyard lies between, Mary —
    My step might break your rest —
Where you, my darling, lie asleep
    With your baby on your breast.

I'm very lonely now, Mary —
    The poor make no new friends; —
But, oh! they love the better still
    The few our Father sends.

And you were all I had, Mary,
    My blessing and my pride;
There's nothing left to care for now
    Since my poor Mary died.

Yours was the good brave heart, Mary,
    That still kept hoping on,
When trust in God had left my soul,
    And half my strength was gone.
There was comfort ever on your lip,
    And the kind look on your brow.
I bless you, Mary, for that same,
    Though you can't hear me now.

I thank you for the patient smile
    When your heart was fit to break;
When the hunger pain was gnawing there
    You hid it for my sake.
I bless you for the pleasant word
    When your heart was sad and sore.
Oh! I'm thankful you are gone, Mary,
    Where grief can't reach you more!

I'm bidding you a long farewell,
    My Mary — kind and true!
But I'll not forget you, darling,
    In the land I'm going to.
They say there's bread and work for all,
    And the sun shines always there;
But I'll not forget old Ireland,
    Were it fifty times as fair.

And when amid those grand old woods
    I sit and shut my eyes,
My heart will travel back again
    To where my Mary lies;

I'll think I see the little stile
    Where we sat, side by side, —
And the springing corn and bright May morn,
    When first you were my bride.

JEREMIAH JOSEPH CALLANAN

The Convict of Clonmel

How hard is my fortune
    And vain my repining;
The strong rope of fate
    For this young neck is twining!
My strength is departed,
    My cheeks sunk and sallow,
While I languish in chains
    In the gaol of Cloonmala.

No boy of the village
    Was ever yet milder;
I'd play with a child
    And my sport would be wilder;
I'd dance without tiring
    From morning 'til even,
And the goal-ball I'd strike
    To the light'ning of Heaven.

At my bed foot decaying
    My hurl-bat is lying;
Through the boys of the village
    My goal-ball is flying;
My horse 'mong the neighbours
    Neglected may fallow,
While I pine in my chains
    In the gaol of Cloonmala.

Next Sunday the patron
  At home will be keeping,
And the young active hurlers
  The field will be sweeping;
With the dance of fair maidens
  The evening they'll hallow,
While this heart once so gay
  Shall be cold in Cloonmala.

JOHN KEEGAN CASEY

The Rising of the Moon

A.D. 1798

'Oh! then tell me, Shawn O'Ferrall,
  Tell me why you hurry so?'
Hush, *mo bhuachaill*, hush and listen,'
  And his cheeks were all aglow.
'I bear orders from the captain,
  Get you ready quick and soon,
For the pikes must be together
  At the risin' of the moon.'

'Oh, then tell me, Shawn O'Ferrall
  Where the gatherin' is to be?'
'In the ould spot by the river,
  Right well known to you and me.
One more word — for signal token
  Whistle up the marching tune,
With your pike upon your shoulder
  By the risin' of the moon.'

Out from many a mud-wall cabin
    Eyes were watching through that night,
Many a manly chest was throbbing
    For the blessed warning light.
Murmurs passed along the valleys
    Like the banshee's lonely croon,
And a thousand blades were flashing
    At the risin' of the moon.

There beside the singing river
    That dark mass of men was seen,
Far above the shining weapons
    Hung their own beloved green.
'Death to every foe and traitor!
    Forward! strike the marching tune,
And hurrah, my boys, for freedom!
    'Tis the risin' of the moon.'

Well they fought for poor old Ireland
    And full bitter was their fate
(Oh! what glorious pride and sorrow
    Fill the name of Ninety-Eight.)
Yet, thank God, e'en still are beating
    Hearts in manhood's burning noon,
Who would follow in their footsteps
    At the risin' of the moon!

AUSTIN CLARKE

Burial of an Irish President

(Dr Douglas Hyde)

The tolling from St Patrick's
Cathedral was brangled, repeating
Itself in top-back room
And alley of the Coombe,
Crowding the dirty streets,
Upbraiding all our pat tricks.
Tricoloured and beflowered,
Coffin of our President,
Where fifty mourners bowed,
Was trestled in the gloom
Of arch and monument,
Beyond the desperate tomb
Of Swift. Imperial flags,
Corunna, Quatre Bras,
Inkermann, Pretoria,
Their pride turning to rags,
Drooped, smoke-thin as the booming
Of cannon. The simple word
From heaven was vaulted, stirred
By candles. At the last bench
Two Catholics, the French
Ambassador and I, knelt down.
The vergers waited. Outside.
The hush of Dublin town,
Professors of cap and gown,
Costello, his Cabinet,
In Government cars, hiding
Around the corner, ready

Tall hat in hand, dreading
Our Father in English. Better
Not hear that 'which' for 'who'
And risk eternal doom.

PÁDRAIC COLUM

The Old Woman of the Roads

Oh to have a little house!
To own the hearth and stool and all!
The heaped-up sods against the fire,
The pile of turf against the wall!

To have a clock with weights and chains,
And pendulum swinging up and down!
A dresser filled with shining delph,
Speckled with white and blue and brown!

I could be busy all the day
Cleaning and sweeping hearth and floor,
And fixing on their shelf again
My white and blue and speckled store!

I could be quiet there at night
Beside the fire and by myself
Sure of a bed and loath to leave
The ticking clock and the shining delph!

Och! but I'm weary of mist and dark,
And roads where there's never a house nor bush,
And tired I am of bog and road,
And the crying wind and the lonesome hush!

And I am praying to God on high,
And I am praying Him night and day,
For a little house — a house of my own —
Out of the wind and the rain's way.

PÁDRAIC COLUM

A Drover

To Meath of the pastures,
From wet hills by the sea,
Through Leitrim and Longford,
Go my cattle and me.

I hear in the darkness
Their slipping and breathing —
I name them the by-ways
They're to pass without heeding;

Then the wet, winding roads,
Brown bogs with black water,
And my thoughts on white ships
And the King o' Spain's daughter.

O farmer, strong farmer!
You can spend at the fair,
But your face you must turn
To your crops and your care;

And soldiers, red soldiers!
You've seen many lands,
But you walk two by two
And by captain's commands!

O the smell of the beasts,
The wet wind in the morn,
And the proud and hard earth
Never broken for corn!

And the crowds at the fair,
The herds loosened and blind,
Loud words and dark faces,
And the wild blood behind!

(O strong men with your best
I would strive breast to breast,
I would quiet your herds
With my words, with my words!)

I will bring you, my kine,
Where there's grass to the knee,
But you'll think of scant croppings
Harsh with salt of the sea.

THOMAS DAVIS

The West's Asleep

When all besides a vigil keep,
The West's asleep, the West's asleep —
Alas! and well may Erin weep,
When Connaught lies in slumber deep.
There lake and plain smile fair and free,
'Mid rocks — their guardian chivalry —
Sing oh! let man learn liberty
From crashing wind and lashing sea.

That chainless wave and lovely land
Freedom and Nationhood demand —
Be sure, the great God never planned,
For slumbering slaves, a home so grand.
And, long, a brave and haughty race
Honoured and sentinelled the place —
Sing oh! not even their sons' disgrace
Can quite destroy their glory's trace.

For often, in O'Connor's van,
To triumph dashed each Connaught clan —
And fleet as deer the Normans ran
Through Corlieu's Pass and Ardrahan.
And later times saw deeds as brave;
And glory guards Clanricard's grave —
Sing oh! they died their land to save,
At Aughrim's slopes and Shannon's wave.

And if, when all a vigil keep,
The West's asleep, the West's asleep —
Alas! and well may Erin weep,
That Connaught lies in slumber deep.
But — hark! — some voice like thunder spake,
"*The West's awake, the West's awake*" —
"Sing oh! hurrah! let England quake,
We'll watch till death for Erin's sake!"

THOMAS DAVIS

My Land

She is a rich and rare land,
Oh she's a fresh and fair land;
She is a dear and rare land,
This native land of mine.

No men than hers are braver,
Her women's hearts ne'er waver;
I'd freely die to save her,
And think my lot divine.

She's not a dull or cold land,
No, she's a warm and bold land,
Oh, she's a true and old land,
This native land of mine.

Could beauty ever guard her,
And virtue still reward her,
No foe would cross her border —
No friend within it pine.

Oh, she's a fresh and fair land,
Oh, she's a true and rare land;
Yes she's a rare and fair land,
This native land of mine.

SIR AUBREY DE VERE

The Rock of Cashel

Royal and saintly Cashel! I would gaze
    Upon the wreck of thy departed powers,
    Not in the dewy light of matin hours,
Nor the meridian pomp of summer's blaze,
But at the close of dim autumnal days,
    When the sun's parting glance, through
    slanting showers,
    Sheds o'er thy rock-throned battlements and towers

Such awful gleams as brighten o'er Decay's
Prophetic cheek. At such a time, methinks,
    There breathes from thy lone courts and
    voiceless aisles
A melancholy moral, such as sinks
    On the lone traveller's heart, amid the piles
Of vast Persepolis on her mountain stand,
Or Thebes half buried in the desert sand.

PAUL DURCAN

On the Floor at the Foot of the Bed

The pyjamas Daddy died in —
St Bernard, Dunnes Stores, 100% Cotton,
Extra Large, To Fit Chest 43–44,
Do Not Soak, Re-Shape While Damp —
I have no problem about wearing them,
No more than you have a problem
About wearing the nightdress
That your mother died in.
It is a little nightdress,
A little ball of white cotton,
And besides, it will not be long
Until I will be ripping it off
Your small, frail body,
Rabbitroutes behind your ears,
And you will be ripping
Daddy's pyjamas
Off my own small, frail body,
Rabbitroutes behind my ears.

I will toss your mother's nightdress
On the floor at the foot of the bed.
You will toss my father's pyjamas
On the floor at the foot of the bed.

While they jostle on the floor with seeming passion
We will jostle with clumsy tenderness upon the pillow.

P A U L   D U R C A N

Going Home to Mayo

Winter 1949

Leaving behind us the alien, foreign city of Dublin
My father drove through the night in an old Ford Anglia,
His five-year-old son in the seat beside him,
The rexine seat of red leatherette,
And a yellow moon peered in through the windscreen.
'Daddy, Daddy,' I cried, 'Pass out the moon,'
But no matter how hard he drove he could not pass out
     the moon.
Each town we passed through was another milestone
And their names were magic passwords into eternity:
Kilcock, Kinnegad, Strokestown, Elphin,
Tarmonbarry, Tulsk, Ballaghaderreen, Ballavarry;
Now we were in Mayo and the next stop was Turlough,
The village of Turlough in the heartland of Mayo,
And my father's mother's house, all oil-lamps and women,
And my bedroom over the public bar below,
And in the morning cattle-cries and cock-crows:
Life's seemingly seamless garment gorgeously rent

By their screeches and bellowings. And in the evenings
I walked with my father in the high grass down by
   the river
Talking with him — an unheard-of thing in the city.

But home was not home and the moon could be no
   more outflanked
Than the daylight nightmare of Dublin city:
Back down along the canal we chugged into the city
And each lock-gate tolled our mutual doom;
And railings and palings and asphalt and traffic-lights,
And blocks after blocks of so-called 'new' tenements —
Thousands of crosses of loneliness planted
In the narrowing grave of the life of the father;
In the wide, wide cemetery of the boy's childhood.

PAUL DURCAN

Backside to the Wind

A fourteen-year-old boy is out rambling alone
By the scimitar shores of Killala Bay
And he is dreaming of a French Ireland,
Backside to the wind.

What kind of village would I now be living in?
French vocabularies intertwined with Gaelic
And Irish women with French fathers,
Backside to the wind.

The Ballina Road would become the Rue de Humbert
And wine would be the staple drink of the people;
A staple diet of potatoes and wine,
Backside to the wind.

Monsieur O'Duffy might be the harbour-master
And Madame O'Duffy the mother of thirteen
Tiny philosophers to overthrow Maynooth,
Backsides to the wind.

Father Molloy might be a worker-priest
Up to his knees in manure at the cattle mart;
And dancing and loving on the streets at evening
Backsides to the wind.

Jean Arthur Rimbaud might have grown up here
In a hillside terrace under the round tower;
Would he, like me, have dreamed of an Arabian Dublin,
Backside to the wind?

Garda Ned MacHale might now be a gendarme
Having hysterics at the crossroads;
Excommunicating male motorists, ogling females,
Backside to the wind.

I walk on, facing the village ahead of me,
A small concrete oasis in the wild countryside;
Not the embodiment of the dream of a boy,
Backside to the wind.

Seagulls and crows, priests and nuns,
Perch on the rooftops and steeples,
And their Anglo-American mores asphyxiate me,
Backside to the wind.

Not to mention the Japanese invasion:
Blunt people as serious as ourselves
And as humourless; money is our God,
Backsides to the wind.

The medieval Franciscan Friary of Moyne
Stands house-high, roofless, by;
Past it rolls a vast asphalt pipe,
Backside to the wind,

Ferrying chemical waste out to sea
From the Asahi synthetic-fibre plant;
Where once monks sang, wage earners slave,
Backsides to the wind.

Run on, sweet River Moy,
Although I end my song; you are
The scales of a salmon of a boy,
Backside to the wind.

Yet I have no choice but to leave, to leave,
And yet there is nowhere I more yearn to live
Than in my own wild countryside,
Backside to the wind.

SAMUEL FERGUSON

The Lark in the Clear Air

Dear thoughts are in my mind
And my soul soars enchanted,
As I hear the sweet lark sing
In the clear air of the day.
For a tender beaming smile
To my hope has been granted,
And tomorrow she shall hear
All my fond heart would say.

I shall tell her all my love,
All my soul's adoration;
And I think she will hear me
And will not say me nay.
It is this that fills my soul
With its joyous elation,
As I hear the sweet lark sing
In the clear air of the day.

OLIVER GOLDSMITH

from

The Deserted Village

Beside yon straggling fence that skirts the way,
With blossomed furze unprofitably gay,
There, in his noisy mansion, skill'd to rule,
The village master taught his little school;
A man severe he was, and stern to view,
I knew him well, and every truant knew;
Well had the boding tremblers learned to trace
The day's disasters in his morning face;
Full well they laugh'd with counterfeited glee,
At all his jokes, for many a joke had he;
Full well the busy whisper circling round,
Conveyed the dismal tidings when he frowned;
Yet he was kind, or if severe in aught,
The love he bore to learning was in fault;
The village all declared how much he knew;
'Twas certain he could write, and cypher too;
Lands he could measure, terms and tides presage,
And even the story ran that he could gauge.

In arguing too, the parson owned his skill,
For e'en tho' vanquished, he could argue still;
While words of learned length, and thundering sound,
Amazed the gazing rustics ranged around,
And still they gazed, and still the wonder grew,
That one small head could carry all he knew.

EVA GORE-BOOTH

The Little Waves of Breffny

The grand road from the mountain goes shining to
    the sea,
And there is traffic on it and many a horse and cart,
But the little roads of Cloonagh are dearer far to me,
And the little roads of Cloonagh go rambling through
    my heart.

A great storm from the ocean goes shouting o'er the hill,
And there is glory in it and terror on the wind,
But the haunted air of twilight is very strange and still,
And the little winds of twilight are dearer to my mind.

The great waves of the Atlantic sweep storming on
    the way,
Shining green and silver with the hidden herring shoal,
But the Little Waves of Breffny have drenched my heart
    in spray,
And the Little Waves of Breffny go stumbling through
    my soul.

GERALD GRIFFIN

Hy-Brazil — the Isle of the Blest

On the ocean that hollows the rocks where ye dwell,
A shadowy land has appeared as they tell;
Men thought it a region of sunshine and rest,
And they call'd it 'O Brazil — the Isle of the Blest'.
From year unto year, on the ocean's blue rim,
The beautiful spectre show'd lovely and dim;
The golden clouds curtain'd the deep where it lay,
And it look'd like an Eden, away, far away.

A peasant, who heard of the wonderful tale,
In the breeze of the Orient loosen'd his sail;
From Ara, the holy, he turned to the west,
For though Ara was holy, O Brazil was blest.
He heard not the voices that call'd from the shore —
He heard not the rising wind's menacing roar:
Home, kindred and safety he left on that day,
And he sped to O Brazil, away, far away!

Morn rose on the deep, and that shadowy Isle
O'er the faint rim of distance reflected its smile;
Noon burn'd on the wave, and that shadowy shore
Seemed lovelily distant, and faint as before:
Lone evening came down on the wanderer's track,
And to Ara again he looked timidly back;
Oh! far on the verge of the ocean it lay,
Yet the Isle of the Blest was away, far away!

Rash dreamer, return! O ye winds of the main,
Bear him back to his old peaceful Ara again!
Rash fool! for a vision of fanciful bliss
To barter the calm life of labour and peace!

The warning of reason was spoken in vain,
He never revisited Ara again;
Night fell on the deep, amidst tempest and spray,
And he died on the waters, away, far away!

To you, gentle friends, need I pause to reveal
The lessons of prudence my verses conceal;
How the phantom of pleasure seen distant in youth,
Oft lures a weak heart from the circle of truth.
All lovely it seems, like that shadowy isle,
And the eye of the wisest is caught by its smile;
But ah! for the heart it has tempted to stray
From the sweet home of duty, away, far away!

Poor friendless adventurer! vainly might he
Look back to green Ara along the wild sea;
But the wanderer's heart has a Guardian above,
Who, though erring, remembers the child of His love.
Oh, who at the proffer of safety would spurn,
When all that He asks is the will to return;
To follow a phantom, from day unto day,
And to die in the tempest, away, far away!

SEAMUS HEANEY

Digging

Between my finger and my thumb
The squat pen rests; snug as a gun.

Under my window, a clean rasping sound
When the spade sinks into gravelly ground:
My father, digging. I look down

Till his straining rump among the flowerbeds
Bends low, comes up twenty years away
Stooping in rhythm through potato drills
Where he was digging.

The coarse boot nestled on the lug, the shaft
Against the inside knee was levered firmly.
He rooted out tall tops, buried the bright edge deep
To scatter new potatoes that we picked
Loving their cool hardness in our hands.

By God, the old man could handle a spade.
Just like his old man.

My grandfather cut more turf in a day
Than any other man on Toner's bog.
Once I carried him milk in a bottle
Corked sloppily with paper. He straightened up
To drink it, then fell to right away
Nicking and slicing neatly, heaving sods
Over his shoulder, going down and down
For the good turf. Digging.

The cold smell of potato mould, the squelch and slap
Of soggy peat, the curt cuts of an edge
Through living roots awaken in my head.
But I've no spade to follow men like them.

Between my finger and my thumb
The squat pen rests.
I'll dig with it.

SEAMUS HEANEY

Blackberry-Picking

Late August, given heavy rain and sun
For a full week, the blackberries would ripen.
At first, just one, a glossy purple clot
Among others, red, green, hard as a knot.
You ate that first one and its flesh was sweet
Like thickened wine: summer's blood was in it
Leaving stains upon the tongue and lust for
Picking. Then red ones inked up and that hunger
Sent us out with milk-cans, pea-tins, jam-pots
Where briars scratched and wet grass bleached our boots.
Round hayfield, cornfields and potato-drills
We trekked and picked until the cans were full,
Until the tinkling bottom had been covered
With green ones, and on top big dark blobs burned
Like a plate of eyes. Our hands were peppered
With thorn pricks, our palms sticky as Bluebeard's.

We hoarded the fresh berries in the byre.
But when the bath was filled we found a fur,
A rat-grey fungus, glutting on our cache.
The juice was stinking too. Once off the bush
The fruit fermented, the sweet flesh would turn sour.
I always felt like crying. It wasn't fair
That all the lovely canfuls smelt of rot.
Each year I hoped they'd keep, knew they would not.

SEAMUS HEANEY

North

I returned to a long strand,
the hammered curve of a bay,
and found only the secular
powers of the Atlantic thundering.

I faced the unmagical
invitations of Iceland,
the pathetic colonies
of Greenland, and suddenly

those fabulous raiders,
those lying in Orkney and Dublin
measured against
their long swords rusting,

those in the solid
belly of stone ships,
those hacked and glinting
in the gravel of thawed streams

were ocean-deafened voices
warning me, lifted again
in violence and epiphany.
The longship's swimming tongue

was buoyant with hindsight —
it said Thor's hammer swung
to geography and trade,
thick-witted couplings and revenges,

the hatred and behindbacks
of the althing, lies and women,
exhaustions nominated peace,
memory incubating the spilled blood.

It said, 'Lie down
in the word-hoard, burrow
the coil and gleam
of your furrowed brain.

Compose in darkness.
Expect aurora borealis
in the long foray
but no cascade of light.

Keep your eye clear
As the bleb of the icicle,
trust the feel of what nubbed treasure
your hands have known.'

SEAMUS HEANEY

The Toome Road

One morning early I met armoured cars
In convoy, warbling along on powerful tyres,
All camouflaged with broken alder branches,
And headphoned soldiers standing up in turrets.
How long were they approaching down my roads
As if they owned them? The whole country was sleeping.
I had rights-of-way, fields, cattle in my keeping,
Tractors hitched to buckrakes in open sheds,
Silos, chill gates, wet slates, the greens and reds
Of outhouse roofs. Whom should I run to tell

Amongst all of those with their back doors on the latch
For the bringer of bad news, that small-hours visitant
Who, by being expected, might be kept distant?
Sowers of seed, erectors of headstones ...
O charioteers, above your dormant guns,
It stands here still, stands vibrant as you pass,
The invisible, untoppled omphalos.

SEAMUS HEANEY

Exposure

It is December in Wicklow:
Alders dripping, birches
Inheriting the last light,
The ash tree cold to look at.

A comet that was lost
Should be visible at sunset,
Those million tons of light
Like a glimmer of haws and rose-hips,

And I sometimes see a falling star.
If I could come on meteorite!
Instead I walk through damp leaves,
Husks, the spent flukes of autumn,

Imagining a hero
On some muddy compound,
His gift like a slingstone
Whirled for the desperate.

How did I end up like this?
I often think of my friends'
Beautiful prismatic counselling
And the anvil brains of some who hate me

As I sit weighing and weighing
My responsible tristia.
For what? For the ear? For the people?
For what is said behind-backs?

Rain comes down through the alders
In low conducive voices
Mutter about let-downs and erosions
And yet each drop recalls

The diamond absolutes.
I am neither internee nor informer;
An inner émigré, grown long-haired
And thoughtful; a wood-kerne

Escaped from the massacre,
Taking protective colouring
From bole and bark, feeling
Every wind that blows;

Who, blowing up these sparks
For their meagre heat, have missed
The once-in-a-lifetime portent,
The comet's pulsing rose.

JOHN KELLS INGRAM

The Memory of the Dead

Who fears to speak of Ninety-Eight?
    Who blushes at the name?
When cowards mock the patriot's fate,
    Who hangs his head for shame?
He's all a knave or half a slave
    Who slights his country thus:
But a true man, like you, man,
    Will fill your glass with us.

We drink the memory of the brave,
    The faithful and the few —
Some lie far off beyond the wave,
    Some sleep in Ireland, too;
All, all are gone — but still lives on
    The fame of those who died;
And true men, like you, men,
    Remember them with pride.

Some on the shores of distant lands
    Their weary hearts have laid,
And by the stranger's heedless hands
    Their lonely graves were made;
But though their clay be far away
    Beyond the Atlantic foam,
In true men, like you, men,
    Their spirit's still at home.

The dust of some is Irish earth;
    Among their own they rest;
And the same land that gave them birth
    Has caught them to her breast;

And we will pray that from their clay
    Full many a race may start
Of true men, like you, men,
    To act as brave a part.

They rose in dark and evil days
    To right their native land;
They kindled here a living blaze
    That nothing shall withstand.
Alas! that Might can vanquish Right —
    They fell, and passed away;
But true men, like you, men,
    Are plenty here today.

Then here's their memory — may it be
    For us a guiding light,
To cheer our strife for liberty,
    And teach us to unite!
Through good and ill, be Ireland's still,
    Though sad as theirs, your fate;
And true men, be you, men,
    Like those of Ninety-Eight.

JAMES JOYCE

Ecce Puer

Written on the birth of his grandson and the death of his father

Of the dark past
A child is born.
With joy and grief
My heart is torn.

Calm in his cradle
The living lies.
May love and mercy
Unclose his eyes!

Young life is breathed
On the glass;
The world that was not
Comes to pass.

A child is sleeping;
An old man gone.
O, father forsaken,
Forgive your son.

JAMES JOYCE

from

The Ballad of Persse O'Reilly

Have you heard of one Humpty Dumpty
How he fell with a roll and a rumble
And curled up like Lord Olofa Crumple
By the butt of the Magazine Wall,
    (Chorus) Of the Magazine Wall,
        Hump, helmet and all?

He was one time our King of the Castle
Now he's kicked about like a rotten old parsnip.
And from Green street he'll be sent by order of His
    Worship
To the penal jail of Mountjoy
    (Chorus) To the jail of Mountjoy!
        Jail him and joy.

He was fafafather of all schemes for to bother us
Slow coaches and immaculate contraceptives for the populace,
Mare's milk for the sick, seven dry Sundays a week,
Openair love and religion's reform,
    (Chorus) And religious reform,
        Hideous in form.

Arrah, why, says you, couldn't he manage it?
I'll go bail, my fine dairyman darling,
Like the bumping bull of the Cassidys
All your butter is in your horns.
    (Chorus) His butter is in his horns.
        Butter his horns!

It was during some fresh water garden pumping
Or, according to the *Nursing Mirror*, while admiring
    the monkeys
That our heavyweight heathen Humpharey
Made bold a maid to woo
    (Chorus) Woohoo, what'll she doo!
        The general lost her maidenloo!

He ought to blush for himself, the old hayheaded
    philosopher,
For to go and shove himself that way on top of her.
Begob, he's the crux of the catalogue
Of our antediluvial zoo,
    (Chorus) Messrs Billing and Coo.
        Noah's larks, good as noo.

He was joulting by Wellinton's monument
Our rotorious hippopopotamuns
When some bugger let down the backtrap of the omnibus
And he caught his death of fusiliers,
    (Chorus) With his rent in his rears.
        Give him six years.

'Tis sore pity for his innocent poor children
But look out for his missus legitimate!
When that frew gets a grip of old Earwicker
Won't there be earwigs on the green?
>   (Chorus) Big earwigs on the green,
>   The largest ever you seen.

>   Suffoclose! Shikespower! Suedodanto! Anonymoses!

Then we'll have a free trade Gaels' band and mass meeting
For to sod the brave son of Scandiknavery.
And we'll bury him down in Oxmanstown
Along with the devil and Danes,
>   (Chorus) With the deaf and dumb Danes,
>   And all their remains.

And not all the king's men nor his horses —
Will resurrect his corpus
For there's no true spell in Connacht or hell
>   (bis) That's able to raise a Cain.

PATRICK KAVANAGH

Shancoduff

My black hills have never seen the sun rising,
Eternally they look north towards Armagh.
Lot's wife would not be salt if she had been
Incurious as my black hills that are happy
When dawn whitens Glassdrummond chapel.

My hills hoard the bright shillings of March
While the sun searches in every pocket.
They are my Alps and I have climbed the Matterhorn
With a sheaf of hay for three perishing calves
In the field under the big Forth of Rocksavage.

The sleety winds fondle the rushy beards of Shancoduff
While the cattle-drovers sheltering in the Featherna Bush
Look up and say: 'Who owns them hungry hills
That the water-hen and snipe must have forsaken?
A poet? Then by heavens he must be poor.'
I hear and is my heart not badly shaken?

PATRICK KAVANAGH

Epic

I have lived in important places, times
When great events were decided, who owned
That half a rood of rock, a no-man's land
Surrounded by our pitchfork-armed claims.
I heard the Duffys shouting 'Damn you soul'
And old McCabe stripped to the waist, seen
Step the plot defying blue-cast steel —
'Here is the march along these iron stones.'
That was the year of the Munich bother. Which
Was more important? I inclined
To lose my faith in Ballyrush and Gortin
Till Homer's ghost came whispering to my mind.
He said: I made the Iliad from such
A local row. Gods make their own importance.

PATRICK KAVANAGH

Canal Bank Walk

Leafy-with-love banks and the green waters of the canal
Pouring redemption for me, that I do
The will of God, wallow in the habitual, the banal,
Grow with nature again as before I grew.
The bright stick trapped, the breeze adding a third
Party to the couple kissing on an old seat,
And a bird gathering materials for the nest for the Word
Eloquently new and abandoned to its delirious beat.
O unworn world enrapture me, encapture me in a web
Of fabulous grass and eternal voices by a beech,
Feed the gaping need of my senses, give me ad lib
To pray unselfconsciously with overflowing speech
For this soul needs to be honoured with a new
    dress woven
From green and blue things and arguments that cannot
    be proven.

PATRICK KAVANAGH

Lines Written on a Seat on the Grand Canal, Dublin, 'Erected to the Memory of Mrs Dermot O'Brien'

O commemorate me where there is water,
Canal water preferably, so stilly
Greeny at the heart of summer. Brother
Commemorate me thus beautifully.
Where by a lock Niagariously roars
The falls for those who sit in the tremendous silence

Of mid-July. No one will speak in prose
Who finds his way to these Parnassian islands.
A swan goes by head low with many apologies,
Fantastic light looks through the eyes of bridges —
And look! a barge comes bringing from Athy
And other far-flung towns mythologies.
O commemorate me with no hero-courageous
Tomb — just a canal-bank seat for the passer-by.

PATRICK KAVANAGH

In Memory of my Mother

I do not think of you lying in the wet clay
Of a Monaghan graveyard; I see
You walking down a lane among the poplars
On your way to the station, or happily

Going to second Mass on a summer Sunday —
You meet me and you say:
'Don't forget to see about the cattle — '
Among your earthiest words the angels stray.

And I think of you walking along a headland
Of green oats in June,
So full of repose, so rich with life —
And I see us meeting at the end of a town

On a fair day by accident, after
The bargains are all made and we can walk
Together through the shops and stalls and markets
Free in the oriental streets of thought.

O you are not lying in the wet clay,
For it is a harvest evening now and we
Are piling up the ricks against the moonlight
And you smile up at us — eternally.

PATRICK KAVANAGH

On Raglan Road

(Air: The Dawning of the Day)

On Raglan Road on an autumn day I met her
    first and knew
That her dark hair would weave a snare that
    I might one day rue;
I saw the danger, yet I walked along the
    enchanted way,
And I said, let grief be a fallen leaf at the dawning
    of the day.

On Grafton Street in November we tripped lightly
    along the ledge
Of the deep ravine where can be seen the worth of
    passion's pledge,
The Queen of Hearts still making tarts and I not
    making hay —
O I loved too much and by such by such is
    happiness thrown away.

I gave her gifts of the mind I gave her the secret
    sign that's known
To the artists who have known the true gods of
    sound and stone

And word and tint. I did not stint for I gave her
    poems to say.
With her own name there and her own dark hair
    like clouds over fields of May.

On a quiet street where old ghosts meet I see her
    walking now
Away from me so hurriedly my reason must allow
That I had wooed not as I should a creature made
    of clay —
When the angel woos the clay he'd lose his wings
    at the dawn of day.

BRENDAN KENNELLY

My Dark Fathers

My dark fathers lived the intolerable day
Committed always to the night of wrong,
Stiffened at the hearthstone, the woman lay,
Perished feet nailed to her man's breastbone.
Grim houses beckoned in the swelling gloom
Of Munster fields where the Atlantic night
Fettered the child within the pit of doom,
And everywhere a going down of light.

And yet upon the sandy Kerry shore
The woman once had danced at ebbing tide
Because she loved flute music — and still more
Because a lady wondered at the pride
Of one so humble. That was long before
The green plant withered by an evil chance;
When winds of hunger howled at every door
She heard the music dwindle and forgot the dance.

Such mercy as the wolf receives was hers
Whose dance became a rhythm in a grave,
Achieved beneath the thorny savage furze
That yellowed fiercely in a mountain cave.
Immune to pity, she, whose crime was love,
Crouched, shivered, searched the threatening sky,
Discovered ready signs, compelled to move
Her to her innocent, appalling cry.

Skeletoned in darkness, my dark fathers lay
Unknown, and could not understand
The giant grief that trampled night and day,
The awful absence moping through the land.
Upon the headland, the encroaching sea
Left sand that hardened after tides of Spring,
No dancing feet disturbed its symmetry
And those who loved good music ceased to sing.

Since every moment of the clock
Accumulates to form a final name,
Since I am come of Kerry clay and rock,
I celebrate the darkness and the shame
That could compel a man to turn his face
Against the wall, withdrawn from light so strong
And undeceiving, spancelled in a place
Of unapplauding hands and broken song.

FRANCIS LEDWIDGE

June

Broom out the floor now, lay the fender by,
And plant this bee-sucked bough of woodbine there,
And let the window down. The butterfly
Floats in upon the sunbeam, and the fair
Tanned face of June, the nomad gypsy, laughs
Above her widespread wares, the while she tells
The farmers' fortunes in the fields, and quaffs
The water from the spider-peopled wells.

The hedges are all drowned in green grass seas
And bobbing poppies flare like Elmo's light,
While siren-like the pollen-stained bees
Drone in the clover depths. And up the height
The cuckoo's voice is hoarse and broke with joy.
And on the lowland crops the crows make raid,
Nor fear the clappers of the farmer's boy,
Who sleeps, like drunken Noah, in the shade.

And loop this red rose in that hazel ring
That snares your little ear, for June is short
And we must joy in it and dance and sing,
And from her bounty draw her rosy worth.
Ay! soon the swallows will be flying south,
The wind wheel north to gather in the snow,
Even the roses spilt on youth's red mouth
Will soon blow down the road all roses go.

FRANCIS LEDWIDGE

Thomas MacDonagh

He shall not hear the bittern cry
In the wild sky, where he is lain,
Nor voices of the sweeter birds
Above the wailing of the rain.

Nor shall he know when loud March blows
Thro' slanting snows her fanfare shrill,
Blowing to flame the golden cup
Of many an upset daffodil.

But when the Dark Cow leaves the moor,
And pastures poor with greedy weeds,
Perhaps he'll hear her low at morn
Lifting her horn in pleasant meads,

LOUIS MACNEICE

The Sunlight on the Garden

The sunlight on the garden
Hardens and grows cold,
We cannot cage the minute
Within its nets of gold,
When all is told
We cannot beg for pardon.

Our freedom as free lances
Advances towards its end;
The earth compels, upon it
Sonnets and birds descend;
And soon, my friend,
We shall have no time for dances.

The sky was good for flying
Defying the church bells
And every evil iron
Siren and what it tells:
The earth compels,
We are dying, Egypt, dying

And not expecting pardon,
Hardened in heart anew,
But glad to have sat under
Thunder and rain with you,
And grateful too
For sunlight in the garden.

DEREK MAHON

A Disused Shed in Co. Wexford

Even now there are places where a thought might grow —
Peruvian mines, worked out and abandoned
To a slow clock of condensation,
An echo trapped for ever, and a flutter
Of wildflowers in the lift-shaft,
Indian compounds where the wind dances
And a door bangs with diminished confidence,
Lime crevices behind rippling rainbarrels,
Dog corners for bone burials;
And in a disused shed in Co. Wexford,

Deep in the grounds of a burnt-out hotel,
Among the bathtubs and the washbasins
A thousand mushrooms crowd to a keyhole.
This is the one star in their firmament

Or frames a star within a star.
What should they do there but desire?
So many days beyond the rhododendrons
With the world waltzing in its bowl of cloud,
They have learnt patience and silence
Listening to the rooks querulous in the high wood.

They have been waiting for us in a foetor
Of vegetable sweat since civil war days,
Since the gravel-crunching, interminable departure
Of the expropriated mycologist.
He never came back, and light since then
Is a keyhole rusting gently after rain.
Spiders have spun, flies dusted to mildew
And once a day, perhaps, they have heard something —
A trickle of masonry, a shout from the blue
Or a lorry changing gear at the end of the lane.

There have been deaths, the pale flesh flaking
Into the earth that nourished it;
And nightmares, born of these and the grim
Dominion of stale air and rank moisture.
Those nearest the door grow strong —
'Elbow room! Elbow room!'
The rest, dim in a twilight of crumbling
Utensils and broken pitchers, groaning
For their deliverance, have been so long
Expectant that there is left only the posture.

A half century, without visitors, in the dark —
Poor preparation for the cracking lock
And creak of hinges. Magi, moonmen,
Powdery prisoners of the old regime,
Web-throated, stalked like triffids, racked by drought
And insomnia, only the ghost of a scream

At the flash-bulb firing squad we wake them with
Shows there is life yet in their feverish forms.
Grown beyond nature now, soft food for worms,
They lift frail heads in gravity and good faith.

They are begging us, you see, in their wordless way,
To do something, to speak on their behalf
Or at least not to close the door again.
Lost people of Treblinka and Pompeii!
'Save us, save us,' they seem to say,
'Let the god not abandon us
Who have come so far in darkness and in pain.
We too had our lives to live.
You with your light meter and relaxed itinerary,
Let not our naive labours have been in vain!'

JAMES CLARENCE MANGAN

Dark Rosaleen

O my Dark Rosaleen,
    Do not sigh, do not weep!
The priests are on the ocean green,
    They march along the Deep.
There's wine ... from the royal Pope
    Upon the ocean green;
And Spanish ale shall give you hope,
    My Dark Rosaleen!
    My own Rosaleen!
Shall glad your heart, shall give you hope,
Shall give you health, and help, and hope,
    My Dark Rosaleen.

Over hills and through dales
    Have I roamed for your sake;
All yesterday I sailed with sails
    On river and lake.
The Erne ... at its highest flood
    I dashed across unseen,
For there was lightning in my blood,
    My Dark Rosaleen!
    My own Rosaleen!
Oh! there was lightning in my blood,
Red lightning lightened through my blood,
    My Dark Rosaleen!

All day long in unrest
    To and fro do I move,
The very soul within my breast
    Is wasted for you, love!
The heart ... in my bosom faints
    To think of you, my Queen,
My life of life, my saint of saints,
    My Dark Rosaleen!
    My own Rosaleen!
To hear your sweet and sad complaints,
My life, my love, my saint of saints,
    My Dark Rosaleen!

Woe and pain, pain and woe,
    Are my lot night and noon,
To see your bright face clouded so,
    Like to the mournful moon.
But yet ... will I rear your throne
    Again in golden sheen;

'Tis you shall reign, shall reign alone,
    My Dark Rosaleen!
    My own Rosaleen!
'Tis you shall have the golden throne,
'Tis you shall reign, and reign alone,
    My Dark Rosaleen!

Over dews, over sands
    Will I fly for your weal;
Your holy delicate white hands
    Shall girdle me with steel.
At home ... in your emerald bowers,
    From morning's dawn till e'en,
You'll pray for me, my flower of flowers,
    My Dark Rosaleen!
    My fond Rosaleen!
You'll think of me through Daylight's hours,
My virgin flower, my flower of flowers,
    My Dark Rosaleen!

I could scale the blue air,
    I could plough the high hills,
Oh, I could kneel all night in prayer,
    To heal your many ills!
And one ... beamy smile from you
    Would float like light between
My toils and me, my own, my true,
    My Dark Rosaleen!
    My fond Rosaleen!
Would give me life and soul anew,
A second life, a soul anew,
    My Dark Rosaleen!

O! the Erne shall run red
    With redundance of blood,
The earth shall rock beneath our tread,
    And flames wrap hill and wood,
And gun-peal, and slogan cry,
    Wake many a glen serene,
Ere you shall fade, ere you shall die,
    My Dark Rosaleen!
    My own Rosaleen!
The Judgement Hour must first be nigh,
Ere you can fade, ere you can die,
    My Dark Rosaleen!

THOMAS MOORE

Let Erin Remember

Let Erin remember the days of old,
Ere her faithless sons betrayed her;
When Malachi wore the collar of gold,
Which he won from her proud invader;
When her kings, with standards of green unfurled,
Led the Red Branch Knights to danger —
Ere the emerald gem of the western world
Was set in the crown of a stranger.

On Lough Neagh's bank as the fisherman strays,
When the clear cold eve's declining,
He sees the round towers of other days
In the wave beneath him shining;
Thus shall memory often, in dreams sublime,
Catch a glimpse of the days that are over;
Thus, sighing, look through the waves of time
For the long-faded glories they cover.

THOMAS MOORE

The Light of Other Days

Oft in the stilly night
Ere slumber's chain has bound me,
Fond memory brings the light
Of other days around me:
The smiles, the tears
Of boyhood's years,
The words of love then spoken;
The eyes that shone,
Now dimmed and gone,
The cheerful hearts now broken!
Thus in the stilly night
Ere slumber's chain has bound me,
Sad memory brings the light
Of other days around me.

When I remember all
The friends so link'd together
I've seen around me fall
Like leaves in wintry weather,
I feel like one
Who treads alone
Some banquet-hall deserted,
Whose lights are fled,
Whose garlands dead
And all but he departed!
Thus in the stilly night
Ere slumber's chain has bound me,
Sad memory brings the light
Of other days around me.

THOMAS MOORE

She is Far from the Land

She is far from the land where her young hero sleeps,
And lovers are round her sighing;
But coldly she turns from their gaze and weeps,
For her heart is in his grave lying.

She sings the wild song of her dear native plains,
Every note which he loved awaking;
Ah! little they think, who delight in their strains,
How the heart of the Minstrel is breaking.

He had lived for his love, for his country he died,
They were all that to life had entwined him;
Nor soon shall the tears of his country be dried,
Nor long will his love stay behind him.

Oh! make her a grave where the sunbeams rest
When they promise a glorious morrow;
They'll shine o'er her sleep, like a smile from the west,
From her own loved island of sorrow.

THOMAS MOORE

The Harp that Once through Tara's Halls

The harp that once through Tara's halls
The soul of music shed,
Now hangs as mute on Tara's walls
As if that soul was fled,
So sleeps the pride of former days,
So glory's thrill is o'er,
And hearts, that once beat high for praise,
Now feel that pulse no more.

No more to chiefs and ladies bright
The harp of Tara swells:
The chord alone, that breaks at night,
Its tale of ruin tells.
Thus Freedom now so seldom wakes,
The only throb she gives
Is when some heart indignant breaks,
To show that she still lives.

NUALA NÍ DHOMHNAILL

I Fall in Love

I fall in love, in the fall of every year,
with the smattering of rain on my windshield
and the pale and wan light toppling over the sheer
edge of my field
of vision, with leaves strewn in my way,
with the bracket-fungus screwed to a rotten log:
I fall in love with bog and cold clay
and what they hold in store for me and you, my dear.

I fall in love with all that's going off:
with blackened spuds
rotting in their beds, with
Brussels sprouts nipped in the bud
by a blast of frost, rat-eaten artichokes, and,
like so many unpicked locks,
the tares and cockles buried in shifting sand;
it's as if I fall in love a little with death itself.

For it's neither the fall nor the coming to in spring —
neither shrug of the shoulders nor sudden foray
down that boring 'little road of the King' —
but something else that makes me wary:
how I throw off the snowy sheet and icy quilt
made of feathers from some flock
of Otherworldly birds, how readily I am beguiled
by a sunny smile, how he offers me a wing.

Original Irish translated by Paul Muldoon

JOHN BOYLE O'REILLY

A White Rose

The red rose whispers of passion,
And the white rose breathes of love;
O, the red rose is a falcon,
And the white rose is a dove.

But I send you a cream-white rosebud,
With a flush on its petal tips;
For the love that is purest and sweetest
Has the kiss of desire on the lips.

EILEEN O'LEARY

from

The Lament for Art O'Leary

My love and my delight,
The day I saw you first
Beside the market-house
I had eyes for nothing else
And love for none but you.

I left my father's house
And ran away with you,
And that was no bad choice;
You gave me everything.
There were parlours whitened for me,
Bedrooms painted for me,
Ovens reddened for me,
Loaves baked for me,
Joints spitted for me,
Beds made for me
To take my ease on flock
Until the milking time
And later if I pleased.

My mind remembers
That bright spring day,
How your hat with its band
Of gold became,
Your silver-hilted sword,
Your manly right hand,
Your horse on her mettle
And foes around you
Cowed by your air;
For when you rode by
On your white-nosed mare
The English lowered their head before you
Not out of love for you
But hate and fear,
For, sweetheart of my soul,
The English killed you.

(Translated from the original Irish by Frank O'Connor)

PATRICK PEARSE

The Wayfarer

The beauty of the world hath made me sad,
This beauty that will pass;
Sometimes my heart hath shaken with great joy
To see a leaping squirrel in a tree,
Or a red lady-bird upon a stalk,
Or little rabbits in a field at evening,
Lit by a slanting sun,
Or some green hill where shadows drifted by,
Some quiet hill where mountainy man hath sown
And soon would reap; near to the gate of Heaven;
Or children with bare feet upon the sands
Of some ebbed sea, or playing on the street
Of little towns in Connacht,
Things young and happy.
And then my heart hath told me:
These will pass,
Will pass and change, will die and be no more,
Things bright and green, things young and happy;
And I have gone upon my way
Sorrowful.

JOSEPH MARY PLUNKETT

The Presence of God

I see His blood upon the rose,
And in the stars the glory of His eyes;
His body gleams amid eternal snows,
His tears fall from the skies.

I see His face in every flower;
The thunder, and the singing of the birds
Are but His voice; and, carven by His power,
Rocks are His written words.

All pathways by His feet are worn;
His strong heart stirs the ever-beating sea;
His crown of thorns is twined with every thorn;
His cross is every tree.

FR PROUT (F.S. MAHONY)

The Shandon Bells

With deep affection
And recollection
I often think of
Those Shandon Bells,
Whose sound so wild would,
In days of childhood,
Fling round my cradle
Their magic spells.
On this I ponder
Where'er I wander
And thus grow fonder,
Sweet Cork, of thee;
With the bells of Shandon
That sound so grand on
The pleasant waters
Of the river Lee.

I've heard bells chiming
Full many a clime in,
Tolling sublime in
Cathedral shrine,
While at a glib rate
Brass tongues would vibrate —
But all their music
Spoke naught like thine;
For memory dwelling
On each proud swelling
Of the belfry knelling
Its bold notes free,
Made the bells of Shandon
Sound far more grand on
The pleasant waters
Of the river Lee.

I've heard bells tolling
Old 'Adrian's Mole' in
Their thunder rolling
From the Vatican,
And Cymbals glorious
Swinging uproarious
In the glorious turrets
Of Notre Dame;
But thy sounds were sweeter
Than the dome of Peter
Flings o'er the Tiber,
Pealing solemnly;
O! the bells of Shandon
Sound far more grand on
The pleasant waters
Of the river Lee.

There's a bell in Moscow,
While on tower and kiosk O!
In Saint Sophia
The Turkman gets,
And loud in air
Calls men to prayer
From the tapering summit
Of tall minarets.
Such empty phantom
I freely grant them;
But there is an anthem
More dear to me —
'Tis the bells of Shandon,
That sound so grand on
The pleasant waters
Of the river Lee.

JAMES STEPHENS

The Snare

I hear a sudden cry of pain!
There is a rabbit in a snare:
Now I hear the cry again,
But I cannot tell from where.

But I cannot tell from where
He is calling out for aid!
Crying on the frightened air,
Making everything afraid!

Making everything afraid!
Wrinkling up his little face!
As he cries again for aid;
— And I cannot find the place!

And I cannot find the place
Where his paw is in the snare!
Little One! Oh, Little One!
I am searching everywhere!

JONATHAN SWIFT

Stella's Birthday

This Day, whate'er the Fates decree,
Shall still be kept with Joy by me:
This Day then let us not be told
That you are sick, and I grown old,
Nor think on our approaching Ills,
And talk of Spectacles and Pills;
Tomorrow will be Time enough
To hear such mortifying Stuff.
Yet since from Reason may be brought
A better and more pleasing Thought,
Which can, in spite of all Decays,
Support a few remaining Days;
From not the gravest of Divines
Accept for once some serious lines.

   Although we now can form no more
Long Schemes of Life as heretofore;
Yet you, while Time is running fast
Can look with Joy on what is past.

   Were Future Happiness and Pain,
A mere Contrivance of the Brain,
As Atheists argue, to entice
And fit their Proselytes for Vice;

(The only Comfort they propose
To have Companions in their Woes).
Grant this the Case, yet sure 'tis hard
That Virtue stil'd its own Reward
And by all Sages understood
To be the chief of human Good,
Should acting, die, nor leave behind
Some lasting Pleasure in the Mind,
Which by Remembrance will assuage
Grief, Sickness, Poverty and Age;
And strongly shoot a radiant Dart
To shine through Life's declining Part.

     Say, *Stella*, feel you no Content
Reflecting on a Life well spent?
Your skilful Hand employ'd to save
Despairing Wretches from the Grave;
And then supporting with your Store
Those whom you dragg'd from Death before
(So Providence on Mortals waits,
Preserving what it just creates)
Your gen'rous Boldness to defend
An innocent and absent Friend;
That Courage which can make you just
To Merit humbled in the Dust:
The Detestation you express
For Vice in all its glitt'ring Dress:
That Patience under tort'ring Pain,
Where stubborn Stoicks would complain.

     Must these like empty Shadows pass,
Or Forms reflected from a Glass?
Or mere Chimaeras in the Mind,
That fly and leave no Marks behind?
Does not the Body thrive and grow

By Food of twenty Years ago?
And, had it not been still supply'd
It must a thousand Times have dy'd:
Then, who with Reason can maintain
That no Effects of Food remain?
And is not Virtue in Mankind
That Nutriment that feeds the Mind?
Upheld by each good Action past,
And still continued by the last:
Then, who with Reason can pretend
That all Effects of Virtue end?

Believe me *Stella*, when you show
That true Contempt for Things below,
Nor prize your Life for other Ends
Than merely to oblige your Friends;
Your former Actions claim their Part,
And join to fortify your Heart.
For Virtue in her daily Race,
Like *Janus*, bears a double Face;
Looks back with Joy where she has gone,
And therefore goes with Courage on.
She at your sickly Couch will wait,
And guide you to a better State.

O then, whatever Heav'n intends,
Take Pity on your pitying Friends;
Nor let your Ills affect your Mind,
To fancy they can be unkind.
Me, surely me, you ought to spare,
Who gladly would your Suff'rings share;
Or give my Scrap of Life to you,
And think it far beneath your Due,
You, to whose Care so oft I owe,
That I'm alive to tell you so.

KATHARINE TYNAN

Sheep and Lambs

All in the April evening,
April airs were abroad;
The sheep with their little lambs
Passed me by on the road.

The sheep with their little lambs
Passed me by on the road;
All in the April evening,
I thought on the Lamb of God.

The lambs were weary, and crying
With a weak, human cry.
I thought on the Lamb of God
Going meekly to die.

Up in the blue, blue mountains
Dewy pastures are sweet;
Rest for the little bodies,
Rest for the little feet.

But for the Lamb of God,
Up on the hill-top green,
Only a cross of shame,
Two stark crosses between.

All in the April evening,
April airs were abroad;
I saw the sheep with their lambs,
And thought on the Lamb of God.

KATHARINE TYNAN

The Wind that Shakes the Barley

There's music in my heart all day,
I hear it late and early,
It comes from fields are far away,
The wind that shakes the barley.

Above the uplands drenched with dew
The sky hangs soft and pearly,
An emerald world is listening to
The wind that shakes the barley.

Above the bluest mountain crest
The lark is singing rarely,
It rocks the singer into rest,
The wind that shakes the barley.

Oh, still through summers and through springs
It calls me late and early.
Come home, come home, come home, it sings,
The wind that shakes the barley.

EDWARD WALSH

The Dawning of the Day

At early dawn I once had been
    Where Lene's blue waters flow,
When summer bid the groves be green,
    The lamp of light to glow.
As on by bower, and town, and tower,
    And widespread fields I stray,
I meet a maid in the greenwood shade
    At the dawning of the day.

Her feet and beauteous head were bare,
    No mantle fair she wore;
But down her waist fell golden hair,
    That swept the tall grass o'er.
With milking-pail she sought the vale,
    And bright her charms' display;
Outshining far the morning star
    At the dawning of the day.

Beside me sat that maid divine
    Where grassy banks outspread.
'Oh, let me call thee ever mine,
    Dear maid,' I sportive said.
'False man, for shame, why bring me blame?'
    She cried, and burst away —
The sun's first light pursued her flight
    At the dawning of the day.

OSCAR WILDE

from

The Ballad of Reading Gaol

He did not wear his scarlet coat,
For blood and wine are red,
And blood and wine were on his hands
When they found him with the dead,
The poor dead woman whom he loved,
And murdered in her bed.

He walked among the Trial Men
In a suit of shabby grey;
A cricket cap was on his head,
And his step seemed light and gay;
But I never saw a man who looked
So wistfully at the day.

I never saw a man who looked
With such a wistful eye
Upon that little tent of blue
Which prisoners call the sky,
And at every drifting cloud that went
With sails of silver by.

I walked, with other souls in pain,
Within another ring,
And was wondering if the man had done
A great or little thing,
When a voice behind me whispered low,
'That fellow's got to swing.'

Dear Christ! the very prison walls
Suddenly seemed to reel,
And the sky above my head became
Like a casque of scorching steel;
And, though I was a soul in pain,
My pain I could not feel.

I only knew what hunted thought
Quickened his step, and why
He looked upon the garish day
With such a wistful eye;
The man had killed the thing he loved,
And so he had to die.

Yet each man kills the thing he loves,
By each let this be heard,
Some do it with a bitter look
Some with a flattering word.
The coward does it with a kiss,
The brave man with a sword.

W.B. YEATS

The Lake Isle of Innisfree

I will arise and go now, and go to Innisfree,
And a small cabin build there, of clay and wattles made:
Nine bean-rows will I have there, a hive for the honey-bee,
And live alone in the bee-loud glade.

And I shall have some peace there, for peace comes
    dropping slow,
Dropping from the veils of the morning to where the
    cricket sings;

There midnight's all a glimmer, and noon a purple glow,
And evening full of the linnet's wings.

I will arise and go now, for always night and day
I hear lake water lapping with low sounds by the shore;
While I stand on the roadway, or on the pavements grey,
I hear it in the deep heart's core.

W.B. YEATS

The Stolen Child

Where dips the rocky highland
Of Sleuth Wood in the lake,
There lies a leafy island
Where flapping herons wake
The drowsy water-rats;
There we've hid our faery vats,
Full of berries
And of reddest stolen cherries.
Come away, O human child!
To the waters and the wild
With a faery, hand in hand,
For the world's more full of weeping than you can understand.

Where the wave of moonlight glosses
The dim grey sands with light,
Far off by furthest Rosses
We foot it all the night,
Weaving olden dances,
Mingling hands and mingling glances
Till the moon has taken flight;
To and fro we leap

And chase the frothy bubbles
While the world is full of troubles
And is anxious in its sleep.
Come away, O human child!
To the waters and the wild
With a faery, hand in hand,
For the world's more full of weeping than you can understand.

Where the wandering water gushes
From the hills above Glencar,
In pools among the rushes
That scarce could bathe a star,
We seek for slumbering trout
And whispering in their ears
Give them unquiet dreams;
Leaning softly out
From ferns that drop their tears
Over the young streams.
Come away, O human child!
To the waters and the wild
With a faery, hand in hand,
For the world's more full of weeping than you can understand.

Away with us he's going,
The solemn-eyed:
He'll hear no more the lowing
Of the calves on the warm hillside
Or the kettle on the hob
Sing peace into his breast,
Or see the brown mice bob
Round and round the oatmeal chest.
For he comes, the human child,
To the waters and the wild
With a faery, hand in hand,
From a world more full of weeping than he can understand.

W.B. YEATS

When You Are Old

When you are old and grey and full of sleep,
And nodding by the fire, take down this book,
And slowly read, and dream of the soft look
Your eyes had once, and of their shadows deep;

How many loved your moments of glad grace,
And loved your beauty with love false or true,
But one man loved the pilgrim soul in you,
And loved the sorrows of your changing face;

And bending down beside the glowing bars,
Murmur, a little sadly, how Love fled
And paced upon the mountains overhead
And hid his face amid a crowd of stars.

W.B. YEATS

The Song of Wandering Aengus

I went out to the hazel wood,
Because a fire was in my head,
And cut and peeled a hazel wand,
And hooked a berry to a thread;
And when white moths were on the wing,
And moth-like stars were flickering out,
I dropped the berry in a stream
And caught a little silver trout.

When I had laid it on the floor
I went to blow the fire aflame,
But something rustled on the floor,
And someone called me by my name:
It had become a glimmering girl
With apple blossom in her hair
Who called me by my name and ran
And faded through the brightening air.

Though I am old with wandering
Through hollow lands and hilly lands,
I will find out where she has gone,
And kiss her lips and take her hands;
And walk among long dappled grass,
And pluck till time and times are done
The silver apples of the moon,
The golden apples of the sun.

W.B. YEATS

He Wishes for the Cloths of Heaven

Had I the heavens' embroidered cloths,
Enwrought with golden and silver light,
The blue and the dim and the dark cloths
Of night and light and the half-light,
I would spread the cloths under your feet:
But I, being poor, have only my dreams;
I have spread my dreams under your feet;
Tread softly because you tread on my dreams.

W.B. YEATS

Red Hanrahan's Song About Ireland

The old brown thorn-trees break in two high over
    Cummen Strand,
Under a bitter black wind that blows from the left hand;
Our courage breaks like an old tree in a black wind
    and dies,
But we have hidden in our hearts the flame out of
    the eyes
Of Cathleen, the daughter of Houlihan.

The wind has bundled up the clouds high over
    Knocknarea,
And thrown the thunder on the stones for all that
    Maeve can say.
Angers that are like noisy clouds have set our hearts abeat;
But we have all bent low and low and kissed the quiet feet
Of Cathleen, the daughter of Houlihan.

The yellow pool has overflowed high up on
    Clooth-na-Bare,
For the wet winds are blowing out of the clinging air;
Like heavy flooded waters our bodies and our blood;
But purer than a tall candle before the Holy Rood
Is Cathleen, the daughter of Houlihan.

W.B. Yeats

No Second Troy

Why should I blame her that she filled my days
With misery, or that she would of late
Have taught to ignorant men most violent ways,
Or hurled the little streets upon the great,
Had they but courage equal to desire?
What could have made her peaceful with a mind
That nobleness made simple as a fire,
With beauty like a tightened bow, a kind
That is not natural in an age like this,
Being high and solitary and most stern?
Why, what could she have done, being what she is?
Was there another Troy for her to burn?

W.B. Yeats

September 1913

What need you, being come to sense,
But fumble in a greasy till
And add the halfpence to the pence
And prayer to shivering prayer, until
You have dried the marrow from the bone?
For men were born to pray and save:
Romantic Ireland's dead and gone,
It's with O'Leary in the grave.

Yet they were of a different kind,
The names that stilled your childish play,
They have gone about the world like wind,
But little time had they to pray

For whom the hangman's rope was spun,
And what, God help us, could they save?
Romantic Ireland's dead and gone,
It's with O'Leary in the grave.

Was it for this the wild geese spread
The grey wing upon every tide;
For this that all that blood was shed,
For this Edward Fitzgerald died,
And Robert Emmet and Wolfe Tone,
All that delirium of the brave?
Romantic Ireland's dead and gone,
It's with O'Leary in the grave.

Yet could we turn the years again,
And call those exiles as they were
In all their loneliness and pain,
You'd cry, 'Some woman's yellow hair
Has maddened every mother's son':
They weighed so lightly what they gave.
But let them be, they're dead and gone,
They're with O'Leary in the grave.

W.B. YEATS

The Wild Swans at Coole

The trees are in their autumn beauty,
The woodland paths are dry,
Under the October twilight the water
Mirrors a still sky;
Upon the brimming water among the stones
Are nine-and-fifty swans.

The nineteenth autumn has come upon me
Since I first made my count;
I saw, before I had well finished,
All suddenly mount
And scatter wheeling in great broken rings
Upon their clamorous wings.

I have looked upon those brilliant creatures,
And now my heart is sore.
All's changed since I, hearing at twilight,
The first time on this shore,
The bell-beat of their wings above my head,
Trod with a lighter tread.

Unwearied still, lover by lover,
They paddle in the cold
Companionable streams or climb the air;
Their hearts have not grown old;
Passion or conquest, wander where they will,
Attend upon them still.

But now they drift on the still water,
Mysterious, beautiful;
Among what rushes will they build,
By what lake's edge or pool
Delight men's eyes when I awake some day
To find they have flown away?

W.B. YEATS

The Stare's Nest by My Window

The bees build in the crevices
Of loosening masonry, and there
The mother birds bring grubs and flies.
My wall is loosening; honey-bees,
Come build in the empty house of the stare.

We are closed in, and the key is turned
On our uncertainty; somewhere
A man is killed, or a house burned,
Yet no clear fact to be discerned:
Come build in the empty house of the stare.

A barricade of stone or of wood;
Some fourteen days of civil war;
Last night they trundled down the road
That dead young soldier in his blood:
Come build in the empty house of the stare.

We had fed the heart on fantasies,
The heart's grown brutal from the fare;
More substance in our enmities
Than in our love; O honey-bees,
Come build in the empty house of the stare.

W.B. YEATS

In Memory of Eva Gore-Booth and Con Markiewicz

The light of evening, Lissadell,
Great windows open to the south,
Two girls in silk kimonos, both
Beautiful, one a gazelle.
But a raving autumn shears
Blossom from the summer's wreath;
The older is condemned to death,
Pardoned, drags out lonely years
Conspiring among the ignorant.
I know not what the younger dreams —
Some vague Utopia — and she seems,
When withered old and skeleton-gaunt,
An image of such politics.
Many a time I think to seek
One or the other out and speak
Of that old Georgian mansion, mix
Pictures of the mind, recall
That table and the talk of youth,
Two girls in silk kimonos, both
Beautiful, one a gazelle.

Dear shadows, now you know it all,
All the folly of a fight
With a common wrong or right.
The innocent and the beautiful
Have no enemy but time;
Arise and bid me strike a match

And strike another till time catch;
Should the conflagration climb,
Run till all the sages know.
We the great gazebo built,
They convicted us of guilt;
Bid me strike a match and blow.

W.B. YEATS

from

Under Ben Bulben

Irish poets, learn your trade,
Sing whatever is well made,
Scorn the sort now growing up
All out of shape from toe to top,
Their unremembering hearts and heads
Base-born products of base beds.
Sing the peasantry, and then
Hard-riding country gentlemen,
The holiness of monks, and after
Porter-drinkers' randy laughter;
Sing the lords and ladies gay
That were beaten into the clay
Through seven heroic centuries;
Cast your mind on other days
That we in coming days may be
Still the indomitable Irishry.

Under bare Ben Bulben's head
In Drumcliff churchyard Yeats is laid.
An ancestor was rector there
Long years ago, a church stands near,

By the road an ancient cross.
No marble, no conventional phrase;
On limestone quarried near the spot
By his command these words are cut:

> *Cast a cold eye*
> *On life, on death.*
> *Horseman, pass by!*

Index of First Lines

A fourteen-year-old boy is out wandering alone   32

All in the April evening   76

All things bright and beautiful   11

At early dawn I once had been   78

Beside yon straggling fence that skirts the way   35

Between my finger and my thumb   38

Broom out the floor now, lay the fender by   56

Dear thoughts are in my mind   34

Even now there are places where a
    thought might grow   58

Four ducks on a pond   17

Had I the heavens' embroidered cloths   84

Have you heard of one Humpty Dumpty   47

He did not wear his scarlet coat   79

He shall not hear the bittern cry   57

How hard is my fortune   21

I do not think of you lying in the wet clay   52

I fall in love, in the fall of every year   66

I have lived in important places, times   50

I hear a sudden cry of pain!   72

I returned to a long strand   41

I see His blood upon the rose   69

I went out to the hazel wood   83

I will arise and go now, and go to Innisfree   80

I'm sitting on the stile, Mary   19

Irish poets, learn your trade   91

It is December in Wicklow   43

Late August, given heavy rain and sun   40

Leafy-with-love banks and the green
    waters of the canal   51

Leaving behind us the alien, foreign city of Dublin   31

Let Erin remember the days of old   63

My black hills have never seen the sun rising   49

My dark fathers lived the intolerable day   54

My love and my delight   67

O commemorate me where there is water   51

O my Dark Rosaleen   60

Of the dark past   46

Oft in the stilly night   64

'Oh! then tell me, Shawn O'Ferrall   22

Oh to have a little house!   25

On Raglan Road on an autumn day I met
    her first and knew   53

On the ocean that hollows the rocks where ye dwell   37

One morning early I met armoured cars   42

Royal and saintly Cashel! I would gaze   29

She is a rich and rare land   28

She is far from the land where her young hero sleeps   65

The beauty of the world hath made me sad   69

The bees build in the crevices   89

The grand road from the mountain goes
    shining to the sea   36

The harp that once through Tara's halls   65

The light of evening, Lissadell   90

The night before Larry was stretched   14

The old brown thorn-trees break in two high
    over Cummen Strand   85

The pyjamas Daddy died in   30

The red rose whispers of passion   67

The sunlight on the garden   57

The tolling from St Patrick's   24

The trees are in their autumn beauty   87

There is a green hill far away   12

There's music in my heart all day   77
This Day, whate'er the Fates decree   73
To Meath of the pastures   26
Up the airy mountain   17
What need you, being come to sense   86
What shall we do for timber?   13
When all besides a vigil keep   27
When you are old and grey and full of sleep   83
Where dips the rocky highland   81
Who fears to speak of Ninety-Eight?   45
Why should I blame her that she filled my days   86
With deep affection   70

Acknowledgments

For permission to reproduce copyright material, grateful acknowledgment is made to the following:

Blackstaff Press and Paul Durcan for 'Going Home to Mayo' and 'Backside to the Wind' from *A Snail in my Prime* (Harvill in association with Blackstaff Press, 1993), and 'On the Floor at the Foot of the Bed' by Paul Durcan;

Bloodaxe Books Ltd and Brendan Kennelly for his poem 'My Dark Fathers', from *A Time for Voice* by Brendan Kennelly (Bloodaxe Books, 1990);

David Higham Associates Ltd for 'Burial of an Irish President' by Austin Clarke;

Faber & Faber for 'Diggin', 'Blackberry-Picking', 'North', 'The Toome Road' and 'Exposure' by Seamus Heaney and 'The Sunlight on the Garden' by Louis MacNeice;

Oxford University Press for 'A Disused Shed in Co. Wexford', © Derek Mahon 1979. Reprinted from *Poems 1962–1978* (1979);

The Society of Authors on behalf of the copyright owner, Mrs Iris Wise, for 'The Snare' by James Stephens.

'Shancoduff', 'Epic', 'Canal Bank Walk', 'Lines Written on a Seat...', 'In Memory of my Mother' and 'On Raglan Road' are reproduced by kind permission of the trustees of the Estate of Patrick Kavanagh, c/o Peter Fallon, Literary Agent, Loughcrew, Oldcastle, Co. Meath, Ireland.

'I Fall in Love' by Paul Muldoon from the Irish of Nuala Ní Dhomhnaill is reproduced by kind permission of the author and Gallery Press. From *The Astrakhan Cloak* (1992).

The Publishers have used their best efforts to trace all copyright holders. They will, however, make the usual and appropriate arrangements with any who may have inadvertently been overlooked and who contact them.